SACRAMENTO PUBLIC LIBRARY
828 "I" Street
Sacramento, CA 95814
5/14

D0788025

OM COLLECTION OF
PUBLIC LIBRARY

Animals
on the Farm

Bison

Aaron Carr

LET'S READ
AV²
BY WEIGL™
ADDED VALUE • AUDIO VISUAL

www.av2books.com

Go to **www.av2books.com**, and enter this book's unique code.

BOOK CODE

H329459

AV² by Weigl brings you media enhanced books that support active learning.

AV² provides enriched content that supplements and complements this book. Weigl's AV² books strive to create inspired learning and engage young minds in a total learning experience.

Your AV² Media Enhanced books come alive with...

Audio
Listen to sections of the book read aloud.

Video
Watch informative video clips.

Embedded Weblinks
Gain additional information for research.

Try This!
Complete activities and hands-on experiments.

Key Words
Study vocabulary, and complete a matching word activity.

Quizzes
Test your knowledge.

Slide Show
View images and captions, and prepare a presentation.

... and much, much more!

Published by AV² by Weigl
350 5th Avenue, 59th Floor   New York, NY 10118
Website: www.av2books.com   www.weigl.com

Copyright ©2014 AV² by Weigl
All rights reserved. No part of this publication may be reproduced, stored in a retrieval system, or transmitted in any form or by any means, electronic, mechanical, photocopying, recording, or otherwise, without the prior written permission of the publisher.

Library of Congress Cataloging-in-Publication Data
Carr, Aaron.
 Bison / Aaron Carr.
   pages cm. -- (Animals on the farm)
 ISBN 978-1-62127-230-4 (hardcover : alkaline paper) -- ISBN 978-1-62127-234-2 (softcover : alkaline paper)
 1. American bison--Juvenile literature. 2. Farm animals--Juvenile literature. I. Title.
 SF401.A45C38 2013
 636.2'92--dc23
                              2012044724

Printed in the United States of America in North Mankato, Minnesota
1 2 3 4 5 6 7 8 9 0   17 16 15 14 13

022013
WEP300113

Senior Editor: Aaron Carr   Art Director: Terry Paulhus

Weigl acknowledges Getty Images as the primary image supplier for this title.

Animals on the Farm
Bison

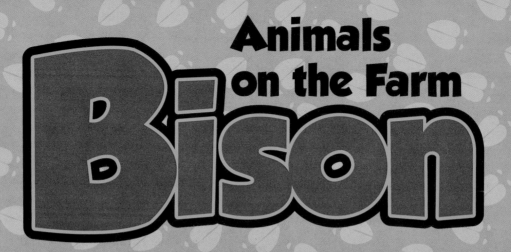

CONTENTS

I am a large farm animal.
Farmers keep me for food.

5

I am a mammal. I have thick fur and a humped back.

I can run very fast.
I like to run with other bison.

I have a large head
with two horns.
My horns help protect me
from other animals.

I eat grass and other plants. In winter, I can find food under the snow. I use my head to push the snow out of the way.

14

I can not see very well.
I use my senses of smell
and hearing instead.

I like to be around other bison.
I live with many bison in a herd.

16

**I have my baby
in the spring or summer.**

My baby is called a calf.

19

My calf will stay with me for three years. It will be full grown after eight years.

BISON FACTS

These pages provide detailed information that expands on the interesting facts found in the book. These pages are intended to be used by adults to help young readers round out their knowledge of each amazing animal featured in the *Animals on the Farm* series.

Pages 4-5

The bison is a large farm animal. People hunted bison for thousands of years. Today, farmers raise bison for their meat, horns, and hides. Bison live outside in large, grassy pastures year-round. Bison farms must have strong fences to keep these large animals from breaking through.

Pages 6–7

Bison are mammals. The bison is the largest land animal in North America. They are related to cattle and oxen. Bison can weigh up to 2,200 pounds (998 kilograms). Male bison, called bulls, can stand up to 6.5 feet (2 meters) tall at the shoulder. Female bison, or cows, are smaller, at 5 feet (1.5 m) tall and up to 1,200 pounds (545 kg).

Pages 8–9

Bison can run very fast. Bison can run at speeds up to 40 miles (65 kilometers) per hour. They often run in large packs, which is called stampeding. In nature, bison migrate north in the spring and south in the fall. Their migration route can cover a distance of 400 miles (640 km).

Pages 10–11

The bison has a big head with two horns. Both male and female bison have horns. The horns curve upward and can be up to 2 feet (61 centimeters) long. Bison keep the same set of horns for life. Male bison bang their heads together to show their strength.

Pages 12–13

Bison eat grass and herbs. They also eat other plants, including leaves and twigs. Bison are ruminants. This means they have four-chambered stomachs. When bison swallow food, it goes to the first chamber. They then regurgitate the food, now called cud, and chew it again. The cud then goes to the second chamber. Food digests as it passes through all four chambers of the stomach.

Pages 14–15

Bison cannot see very well. The bison's eyes are located on each side of its head. This gives the bison about a 330-degree field of vision. This eye location makes it hard for bison to judge distance. The bison makes up for its poor eyesight with excellent senses of hearing and smell. A bison can smell something from about 2 miles (3 km) away.

Pages 16–17

Bison like to live with many other bison. Bison are herd animals. They like to stay together in large numbers. Male and female bison often live in separate groups. During the summer, the male and female bison groups come together to form a large herd.

Pages 18–19

Bison have their babies in the spring or summer. Mothers give birth to a single calf after a nine-month pregnancy. Twin births are rare. Calves weigh about 50 pounds (23 kg) when born, and have a reddish-yellow coat. As they grow, the coat turns brown.

Pages 20–21

A bison calf stays with its mother for three years. Bison calves can run within a few hours of birth. After three or four years, they are able to take care of themselves and have their own babies. Bison continue growing until they are about eight years old. Bison can live up to 25 years.

KEY WORDS

Research has shown that as much as 65 percent of all written material published in English is made up of 300 words. These 300 words cannot be taught using pictures or learned by sounding them out. They must be recognized by sight. This book contains 49 common sight words to help young readers improve their reading fluency and comprehension. This book also teaches young readers several important content words. These words are paired with pictures to aid in learning and improve understanding.

Page	Sight Words First Appearance
4	a, am, animal, farm, food, for, I, keep, large, me
6	and, back, have
8	can, like, other, run, to, very, with
10	from, head, help, my, two
13	eat, find, in, of, out, plants, the, under, use, way
15	not, see, well
16	around, be, live, many
18	or
19	is
20	after, it, three, will, years

Page	Content Words First Appearance
4	farmers
6	fur, mammal
8	bison
10	horns
13	grass, snow, winter
15	hearing, senses, smell
16	herd
18	baby, spring, summer
19	calf

Check out www.av2books.com for activities, videos, audio clips, and more!

1 Go to www.av2books.com.

2 Enter book code. | H329459 |

3 Fuel your imagination online!

www.av2books.com

24